Paid for by donations

from the

Mount Laurel Community

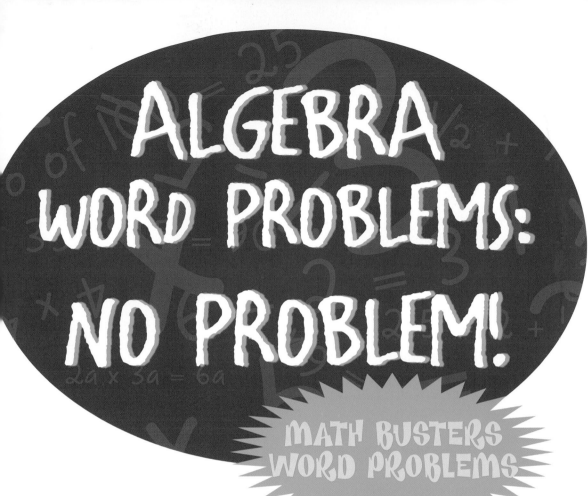

ALGEBRA WORD PROBLEMS: NO PROBLEM!

MATH BUSTERS WORD PROBLEMS

Rebecca Wingard-Nelson

NEED MORE PRACTICE?
free worksheets available at
http://www.enslow.com

Enslow Publishers, Inc.
40 Industrial Road
Box 398
Berkeley Heights, NJ 07922
USA
http://www.enslow.com

Library of Congress Cataloging-in-Publication Data

Wingard-Nelson, Rebecca.
Algebra word problems : no problem! / Rebecca Wingard-Nelson.
    p. cm. — (Math busters word problems)
Summary: "Presents a step-by-step guide to understanding word problems with algebra"—
Provided by publisher.
 Includes bibliographical references and index.
 ISBN 978-0-7660-3367-2
1. Algebra—Juvenile literature. 2. Word problems (Mathematics)—Juvenile literature.   I. Title.
QA155.15.W563 2011
512.0076—dc22
                                   2009037893

Printed in the United States of America

042010 Lake Book Manufacturing, Inc., Melrose Park, IL

10 9 8 7 6 5 4 3 2 1

To Our Readers: We have done our best to make sure all Internet Addresses in this book were active and appropriate when we went to press. However, the author and the publisher have no control over and assume no liability for the material available on those Internet sites or on other Web sites they may link to. Any comments or suggestions can be sent by e-mail to comments@enslow.com or to the address on the back cover.

✪ Enslow Publishers, Inc., is committed to printing our books on recycled paper. The paper in every book contains 10% to 30% post-consumer waste (PCW). The cover board on the outside of each book contains 100% PCW. Our goal is to do our part to help young people and the environment too!

Illustration credits: © Comstock/PunchStock, pp. 5, 7, 18, 21, 46, 50, 53, 60; © Shutterstock, pp. 9, 11, 12, 14, 17, 23, 24, 26, 29, 30, 32, 35, 36, 38, 39, 40, 43, 45, 48, 55, 57, 58.

Cover Photo: Shutterstock

Free Worksheets are available for this book at http://www.enslow.com. Search on the ***Math Busters Word Problems*** series name. The publisher will provide access to the worksheets for five years from the book's first publication date.

Contents

When you hand a cashier a twenty-dollar bill to pay for a pair of socks, you're living in a word problem! Math is everywhere; you just might not realize it all the time because math isn't always written as a math problem.

This book will help you understand how algebra is used in word problems. The step-by-step method can help students, parents, teachers, and tutors solve any word problem. It can be read from beginning to end or used to review a specific topic. Let's get started!

When faced with a word problem, you many think, "How do I start? What do I do if I get stuck? What if the answer is wrong when I check it? Word problems are hard!" Here are some tips.

Get Involved!

You can watch a swim meet and see swimmers racing across a pool. But if you want to *learn* how to swim, you must get in the water. Solving math problems is not a spectator sport. You may first watch how others solve word problems, but then you need to solve them for yourself, too. Go ahead, jump in!

Practice!

Even the most gifted athlete or musician will tell you that in order to play well, you must practice. The more you practice anything, the better and faster you become at it. The same is true for problem solving. Homework problems and class work are your practice.

Learning Means <u>Not</u> Already Knowing!

If you already know everything, there is nothing left to learn. Every mistake you make is a potential learning experience. When you understand a problem and get the right answer the first time, good for you! When you do NOT understand a problem but figure it out, or you make a mistake and learn from it, AWESOME for you!

Questions, Questions!

Ask smart questions. Whoever is helping you does not know what you don't understand unless you tell them. You must ask a question before you can get an answer.

Ask questions early. Concepts in math build on each other. Today's material is essential for understanding tomorrow's.

Don't Give Up!

Stuck on homework? There are many resources for homework help.
* Check a textbook.
* Ask someone who does understand.
* Try looking up sources on the Internet (but don't get distracted).
* Read this book!

Getting frustrated? Take a break.
* Get a snack or a drink of water.
* Move around and get your blood flowing. Then come back and try again.

Stuck on a test? If you do get stuck on a problem, move on to the next one. Solve the problems you understand first. That way, you won't miss the problems you do understand because you were stuck on one you didn't. If you have time, go back and try the ones you skipped.

Wrong answer? Check the math; it could be a simple mistake. Try solving the problem another way. There are many problem-solving strategies, and usually more than one of them will work. Don't give up. If you quit, you won't learn anything.

② Problem-Solving Steps

Solving math word problems can be broken down into four steps. You are more likely to get a correct answer and have less trouble finding it when you follow these steps.

Problem-Solving Steps

Step 1: Understand the problem.
Step 2: Make a plan.
Step 3: Follow the plan.
Step 4: Review.

Step 1: Understand the problem.

Read the problem. Read the problem again. This may seem obvious, but this step may be the most important.

Ask yourself questions like:
Do I understand all of the words in the problem?
Can I restate the problem in my own words?
Will a picture or diagram help me understand the problem?
What does the problem ask me to find or show?
What information do I need to solve the problem? Do I have all of the information?

Underlining the important information can help you to understand the problem. Read the problem as many times as it takes for you to have a clear sense of what happens in the problem and of what you are asked to find.

Step 2: Make a plan.

There are many ways to solve a math problem. Choosing a good plan becomes easier as you solve more problems. Some plans you may choose are:

Make a list.	*Guess and check.*
Draw a picture.	*Work backward.*
Use logical reasoning.	*Solve a simpler problem.*
Use what you know.	*Use a number line or graph.*
Use a model.	*Use a table.*

In algebra, one of the most important plans is **write an equation**. When this is the plan, the main task at this step is to choose the correct operation.

Step 3: Follow the plan.

Now that you understand the problem and have decided how to solve it, you can carry out your plan. Use the plan you have chosen. If it does not work, go back to step 2 and choose a different plan.

Step 4: Review.

Look over the problem and your answer. Does the answer match the question? Does the answer make sense? Is it reasonable? Check the math. What plan worked or did not work? Looking back at what you have done on this problem will help you solve similar problems.

③ Integers

Salem County school district cancels school when the temperature is 10 degrees or more below zero Fahrenheit. The temperature today is 12 degrees below zero Fahrenheit. What integer represents today's temperature?

Step 1: Understand the problem.

Read the problem. Are there any words you do not understand? What does the word *integer* mean?
Integers are whole numbers and their opposites.

What does the problem ask you to find?
The integer that represents today's temperature.

What information do you need to solve the problem? Is all of the information that you need in the question? Is there extra information?
You need to know today's temperature. The information is in the question. You do not need to know that the school district cancels school when the temperature is 10 degrees or more below zero Fahrenheit. That is extra information.

Step 2: Make a plan.

This question asks how you can write the temperature as an integer. It does not ask you to perform any operations. Use what you know about integers and the given temperature to solve the problem.

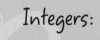

Integers:

Whole numbers and their opposites.

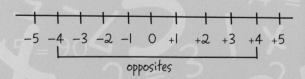

-5 -4 -3 -2 -1 0 +1 +2 +3 +4 +5

opposites

Step 3: Follow the plan.

You know the temperature today is 12 degrees below zero . You know integers are whole numbers and their opposites. To represent a number that is below, or less than zero, use a negative integer.

12 degrees below zero Fahrenheit can be represented by the integer –12.

Step 4: Review.

Does the answer match the question?
Yes, the problem asked for an integer.

Does the answer make sense? **Yes.**

Is it reasonable? **Yes.**

Did the plan work for the problem? **Yes.**

④ Comparing Numbers

Keith and Lori each have 20 words to translate for their Spanish homework. Keith has translated 1/2 of the words so far, and Lori has translated 3/5 of the words. Which student has completed more of the Spanish homework?

Step 1: Understand the problem.

Read the problem. Is there anything you do not understand?

What does the problem ask you to find?
Which student has completed more of the Spanish homework.

What information do you need to solve the problem? Is all of the information that you need in the question? Is there extra information?
You need to know how much of the homework each student has completed. The information is given in the question as a fractional amount for each student. You do not need to know that there are 20 words to translate. That is extra information.

Step 2: Make a plan.

This question asks which student has completed more of the homework. This is a comparison question; there are no operations to perform. Compare the two fractions to see which is larger. One way to compare fractions is to write each fraction with the same denominator.

Step 3: Follow the plan.

Keith has translated 1/2 of the words. Lori has translated 3/5 of the words. The lowest common denominator is 10.

$$\frac{1}{2} \quad \frac{1 \times 5}{2 \times 5} \quad \frac{5}{10} \qquad\qquad \frac{3}{5} \quad \frac{3 \times 2}{5 \times 2} \quad \frac{6}{10}$$

6/10 is greater than 5/10. 3/5 is greater than 1/2. Who has translated 3/5 of the words? Lori.

Lori has completed more of the Spanish homework than Keith.

··

Step 4: Review.

Does the answer match the question?
Yes, the problem asked for a student, and the answer is a student.

Did the plan work for the problem? **Yes.**

Is there another plan you could use? **Yes. You could use fraction bars or a number line to compare the fractions.**

1/2 and 3/5 are rational numbers.

Rational numbers are numbers that can be written as fractions.

Whole numbers, integers, decimals, and fractions are all rational numbers.

Let's use fraction bars to check your answer.

3/5 is greater than 1/2.

Is the answer the same?
Yes.

Sierra has a balance of negative $4 on her lunch account. She puts $10 more into the account. What is Sierra's new account balance?

Step 1: Understand the problem.

Read the problem. Is there anything you do not understand? What kind of integer represents a negative balance?
A negative integer.
What kind of integer represents adding money to an account?
A positive integer.

What does the problem ask you to find?
Sierra's new lunch account balance.

What information do you need to solve the problem? Is all of the information that you need in the question? Is there extra information? **You need to know how much is in the account at the start and how much is added to the account. The information is in the question. There is no extra information.**

Step 2: Make a plan.

This problem starts with an account balance, then more is added to the account. Problems that use words like *increase, more, sum,* or *combined* may be addition problems. Addition problems take two or more values and combine them. You can use a number line to add money to the starting balance. On a number line, to add a positive number move right. To add a negative number, move left.

Step 3: Follow the plan.

The balance at the start of the problem can be represented by the integer −4. The amount Sierra added to the account can be represented by the integer +10.

On a number line, begin at the starting balance, −4. Add the positive integer +10 by moving right 10 units.

You end on +6.

Sierra's new account balance is positive $6.

Step 4: Review.

Does the answer match the question?
Yes. The problem asked for the new account balance.

Does the answer make sense? **Yes. Sierra owed money on her lunch account. She put more money into the account than what she owed. The new balance is positive, but less than the amount she added to the account.**

Did the plan work for the problem? **Yes.**

Is there another plan you could use? **Yes. You could solve an equation. ⁻4 + ⁺10 = ⁺6. The answers, $6, are the same.**

Jamison's football team had a loss of 8 yards in one play. On the same play, a penalty was called that cost them another 5 yards. What integer represents the total loss on the play?

Step 1: Understand the problem.

Read the problem. Is there anything you do not understand? What kind of integer represents a loss? **A negative integer.** What kind of integer represents the penalty? **A negative integer.**

What does the problem ask you to find? **An integer to represent the total loss on the play.**

What information do you need to solve the problem? Is all of the information that you need in the question? Is there extra information? **You need to know how many yards were lost on the play and how many yards are the penalty. The information is in the question. There is no extra information.**

Step 2: Make a plan.

This problem asks for a total loss. You can add the loss of yards from the play and the loss of yards from the penalty using an equation.

Step 3: Follow the plan.

An 8-yard loss can be represented by the integer –8. The loss due to the penalty can be represented by the integer –5. Add the integers –8 and –5.

–8 + –5 = –13

The total loss can be represent by the integer –13.

Step 4: Review.

Does the answer match the question?
Yes. The problem asked for an integer.

Does the answer make sense? **Yes.
The integer represents a loss,
and the answer is negative.**

Did the plan work for
the problem? **Yes.**

Integers with the
same sign
(positive, +, or negative, −)
are called like integers.

To add like integers, ignore the signs,
add the digits, then use the same sign
as the addends for the sum.

$$-8 + -5 = -13$$

$$+8 + +5 = +13$$

Ethan paid $50 for tickets to the prom. He paid $81 to rent a tuxedo and another $19 for flowers. How much did Ethan pay in all?

Step 1: Understand the problem.

Read the problem. Is there anything you do not understand?

What does the problem ask you to find? **How much Ethan paid in all.**

What information do you need to solve the problem? **Sometimes questions ask for "how much in all" or "how much altogether." These problems want you to add all of the values mentioned in the problem. Do not make the problem harder than it is by thinking of other items that may have been included for a prom, like dinner or a limo ride.**

Is there any extra information? **No, there is no extra information.**

Step 2: Make a plan.

The problem gives you three values: cost of prom tickets, cost of the tuxedo rental, and cost of flowers. To find the value in all, you can add.

Step 3: Follow the plan.

The prom tickets were $50, the tuxedo was $81, and the flowers were $19. Add the three values.

The associative property of addition says that you can add any two addends first, then add the third. In this problem, $81 and $19 can be added easily first because the digits in the ones place total 10 (81 + 19 = 100). Then add the $50 (100 + 50 = 150).

$50 + ($81 + $19) = $150

Ethan paid $150 in all.

Step 4: Review.

Does the answer match the question?
Yes. The problem asked for a dollar amount.

Check the answer by adding in a different order. Add 50 + 81 first, then 19. 50 + 81 = 131. 131 + 19 = 150. Is the answer the same? **Yes.**

Addition Properties

The associative property is one of the four addition properties you can use to make addition problems easier.

The Associative Property: Changing the grouping of addends does not change the sum.

$$(3 + 2) + 1 = 3 + (2 + 1)$$

The Commutative Property: Changing the order of the addends does not change the sum.

$$6 + 1 = 1 + 6$$

The Inverse Property: The sum of opposites is zero.

$$(3) + (^-3) = 0$$

The Zero Property: The sum of a number and zero is the number.

$$12 + 0 = 12$$

⑧ Expressions

Each rectangular table in the food court seats 6 people. Each round table seats 2. Write a numeric expression to find how many people total can sit at one rectangular and one round table.

Step 1: Understand the problem.

Read the problem. Is there anything you do not understand?

What does the problem ask you to find?
An expression to find how many people can sit at one rectangular table and one round table.

What information do you need to solve the problem? **You need to know the number of people who can sit at each type of table.**

Is there any extra information? **No, there is no extra information.**

Expressions

An **expression** stands for a number. Expressions can be numbers, such as 18 or 400. Expressions can also be letters, such as *n* or *t*, that represent unknown numbers. These letters are called **variables**. Expressions can also use operations to show numbers, such as 3 + 2, or *t* − 7.

Expressions that do not use variables are called **numeric expressions**. Expressions that use a variable are called **algebraic expressions** or **variable expressions**.

Step 2: Make a plan.

The problem is asking for an expression. You do not need to perform any operations. To write an expression, you can write what happens in the problem using words, then change the words to numbers and operation symbols.

Step 3: Follow the plan.

The words *and* and *total* tell you this is addition. Use words to tell what is being added.

seats at rectangular table and seats at round table

Now replace the words with numbers and operation symbols.

seats at rectangular table **and** **seats at round table**

6 + 2

Step 4: Review.

Does the answer match the question?
Yes. The problem asked for an expression.

Did the plan work for the problem? **Yes.**

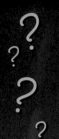

John has saved $1,200 to buy his first car. His grandpa is also giving him some money for the car. Write a variable expression for the total amount of money John can spend on his first car.

Step 1: Understand the problem.

Read the problem. Is there anything you do not understand?

What does the problem ask you to find?
A variable expression for the amount of money John can spend on his first car.

What information do you need to solve the problem?
The amount John has saved, and the amount his grandfather is giving him. The problem does not tell you the amount his grandfather is giving him, so that value will be represented by a variable.

Is there any extra information? **No, there is no extra information.**

Step 2: Make a plan.

The problem is asking for a variable expression. You do not need to perform any operations. Write what happens in the problem using words, then change the words to numbers, variables, and operation symbols.

Step 3: Follow the plan.

The word *total* tells you this is addition. Use words to tell what is being added.

money John has saved and money from grandpa

Now replace the words with numbers, operation symbols, and variables. Since you do not know the amount John's grandpa is giving him, use the variable g to represent that amount.

money John has saved and **money from grandpa**
$$\$1{,}200 + g$$

Step 4: Review.

Does the answer match the question?
Yes. The problem asked for a variable expression.

Did the plan work for the problem? **Yes.**

⑩ Writing Addition Equations

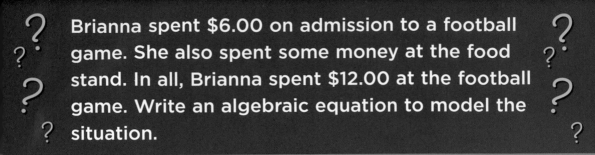

? ? ? ? ?   Brianna spent $6.00 on admission to a football game. She also spent some money at the food stand. In all, Brianna spent $12.00 at the football game. Write an algebraic equation to model the situation.   ? ? ? ? ?

Step 1: Understand the problem.

Read the problem. Is there anything you do not understand?

What does the problem ask you to find?
An algebraic equation to model the situation.

What is the situation?
Brianna spent $6.00 to get into a football game.
She spent some more money at the food stand.

Is there any extra information? **No, there is no extra information.**

Equations

An **equation** uses an equal sign to show that two expressions have the same value. Numeric equations use numbers, operation symbols, and the equal sign. These are the equations, such as 1 + 2 = 3, that you are already familiar with.

Algebraic equations are equations that use a variable instead of a blank line to represent an unknown value.

$$7 + 6 = \text{\_\_\_\_} \text{ as an algebraic equation is } 7 + 6 = a$$
$$3 + \text{\_\_\_\_} = 8 \text{ as an algebraic equation is } 3 + x = 8$$

Step 2: Make a plan.

This problem begins with a value, then adds some more for a total. It is an addition problem. The answer will be an addition equation. Write what happens in the problem using words, then change the words to numbers, variables, and operation symbols.

Step 3: Follow the plan.

Use words to tell what is being added.

admission plus food stand equal total

Now replace the words with numbers, units, operation symbols, and variables. Since you do not know the amount Brianna spent at the food stand, use the variable f to represent that amount.

admission + food stand = total
$$\$6.00 + f = \$12.00$$

Step 4: Review.

Does the answer match the question?
Yes. The problem asked for an algebraic equation. The answer has a variable and an equal sign.

Did the plan work for the problem? **Yes.**

Coach had the entire track team run 4 laps. When they finished, he had the distance runners run some more laps. Each distance runner ran 40 laps in all. Use an algebraic equation to find how many laps the distance runners ran after the rest of the team had finished running.

Step 1: Understand the problem.

Read the problem. Is there anything you do not understand?

What does the problem ask you to find?
The number of laps the distance runners ran after the rest of the team had finished running.

Do you have all of the information you need to solve the problem?
Yes. You know how far the entire team ran and how far the distance runners ran in all.

Does the problem ask for anything else? **Yes. You need to use an algebraic equation to find the answer.**

Step 2: Make a plan.

This problem tells you the plan. You must write an algebraic equation, then solve the equation to find the answer.

Solving Algebraic Equations

The solution to an algebraic equation is the number that makes the equation correct. In the algebraic equation $1 + 2 = c$, the solution is $c = 3$, because $1 + 2 = 3$.

To find the solution to an algebraic equation, get the variable by itself on one side of the equal sign using the properties of equality. The **properties of equality** say that you can perform any operation to both sides of an equation and the equation will still be true.

Step 3: Follow the plan.

The distance runners run with the team, then run some more. This is an addition situation. Use words to tell what happens in the problem. Replace the words with numbers, symbols, and variables. Use the variable r to represent the number of laps the distance runners ran after the rest of the team had finished.

laps run with team plus more laps run = laps run in all

$$4 + r = 40$$

Subtract 4 from each side of the equation to get the variable, r, by itself. Then do the operations.

$$4 + r = 40$$
$$4 - 4 + r = 40 - 4$$
$$r = 36$$

The distance runners ran 36 more laps after the rest of the team had finished running.

Step 4: Review.

Check your answer. **You can check the answer to an algebraic equation by writing the equation and replacing the variable with the solution.**

$$4 + r = 40$$
$$4 + 36 = 40$$
$$40 = 40$$

Jim can buy an MP3 player with 80 GB of space for $247, or he can buy the same brand of MP3 player with 120 GB of space for $326. How much more does the 120-GB MP3 player cost?

Step 1: Understand the problem.

Read the problem. Is there anything you do not understand?

What does the problem ask you to find?
How much more the 120-GB MP3 player costs than the 80-GB MP3 player.

What information do you need to solve the problem? Is all of the information that you need in the question? **You need to know the price of each MP3 player. The information is in the question.**

Is there extra information? **Although there is no extra information, be careful when other numbers are in the problem. The numbers 80 and 120 represent the amount of space on each MP3 player, but are NOT values that are needed to find the solution.**

Step 2: Make a plan.

Problems that ask for a difference between values are subtraction problems. Problems that use words like *how much more or less, how many more or less,* or *difference* may be subtraction problems.

Some subtraction problems may start with a value, and then have part taken away. Words like *left, take away, less than, fewer,* or *remain* may also tell you to use subtraction. You can use an equation to solve this problem.

Step 3: Follow the plan.

To find a difference between two values, begin with the larger value, $326, and subtract the smaller value, $247.

$$\begin{array}{r} \$326 \\ -\ \$247 \\ \hline \$\ \ 79 \end{array}$$

The 120-GB MP3 player costs $79 more than the 80-GB MP3 player.

....

Step 4: Review.

Does the answer match the question? **Yes. The problem asked how much more, which is a dollar value.**

Check the answer. **Subtraction problems can be checked using addition. Add the answer and the value that was subtracted. The sum should be the starting value.**

$79 + $247 = $326

Brijesh borrowed $16.80 from Kari to buy a book about baseball. Then he borrowed another $4.75 to buy a cappuccino. He gave her back $20.00 when they returned home. Does Brijesh still owe Kari money? If so, how much?

Step 1: Understand the problem.

Read the problem. Is there anything you do not understand?

What does the problem ask you to find?
Whether Brijesh still owes Kari money and, if so, how much.

What information do you need to solve the problem? Is all of the information that you need in the question? **You need to know how much money Brijesh borrowed from Kari, and how much he paid her back. The information is in the question.**

Is there extra information? **No, there is no extra information.**

Step 2: Make a plan.

You may break some problems into smaller parts.
Break this problem into two parts. First, add to find the total amount Brijesh borrowed. Then compare the amount he borrowed to the amount he paid Kari back. If Brijesh still owes Kari money, subtract to find how much he owes her.

Step 3: Follow the plan.

Add the total amount Brijesh borrowed.

Book	$16.80
Cappuccino	+ $ 4.75
Total	$21.55

Compare the amount Brijesh borrowed, $21.55, to the amount he paid back, $20.00. He borrowed more than he paid back.

Yes, Brijesh still owes Kari money.

Subtract to find the amount Brijesh still owes Kari.

Borrowed	$21.55
Paid	- $20.00
Still Owes	$ 1.55

Brijesh still owes Kari $1.55.

Step 4: Review.

Does the answer match the question?
Yes. The problem asked if Brijesh still owed Kari money and, if so, how much. There are two questions and two answers.

Did the plan work for the problem? **Yes.**

Brice's average in Spanish class went down 12 points from the first marking period to the second marking period to 82. Use an algebraic equation to find Brice's average in Spanish class during the first marking period.

Step 1: Understand the problem.

Read the problem. Is there anything you do not understand?

What does the problem ask you to find?
Brice's average in Spanish class during the first marking period.

Do you have all of the information you need to solve the problem?
Yes. You know the second marking period average and the amount the grade changed.

Does the problem ask for anything else? **Yes. You need to use an algebraic equation to find the answer.**

Step 2: Make a plan.

This problem tells you the plan. You must write an algebraic equation, then solve the equation to find the answer.

Step 3: Follow the plan.

Brice has an average grade, then it goes down. This is a subtraction situation. Use words to tell what happens in the problem. Replace the words with numbers, symbols, and variables. Use the variable f to represent the average in Spanish for the first marking period.

first marking period average minus points the average went down = second marking period average

$$f - 12 = 82$$

Add 12 to each side of the equation to get the variable, f, by itself. Then do the addition.

$$f - 12 = 82$$
$$f - 12 + 12 = 82 + 12$$
$$f = 94$$

Brice had a 94% average in Spanish class for the first marking period.

....

Step 4: Review.

Check your answer. **Try testing the answer in the context of the problem. If Brice had a 94% average in Spanish for the first marking period, and his average went down 12 points, then his second marking period average was**
$$94 - 12 = 82$$

ERROR ALERT:

"less than"

When you need to change words such as "2 less than x," you may want to write "2 - x." DON'T!
Look at this "real world" situation, and you'll see how this is wrong: "His age is 2 years less than mine." You do NOT figure his age by subtracting your age from 2. Instead, you subtract 2 from your age, "x - 2."

Erin sees one new movie at the Saturday matinee price every weekend. How much did she spend to see new movies over 6 weekends?

Adult:
$8.00
Child ages 3-12:
$6.00
Senior:
$5.00
Saturday
Matinee—All:
$5.00

Step 1: Understand the problem.

Read the problem. Is there anything you do not understand? What is a matinee? **The word *matinee* comes from the French word for "morning." In this case, a matinee is a movie that is shown in the morning or early afternoon. To solve the problem, you do not need to know what a matinee is, just that it has a different price than other movie tickets.**

What does the problem ask you to find?
How much Erin spent to see matinee movies over 6 weekends.

What information do you need to solve the problem? **You need to know how many new movies Erin saw, and the price to see each movie.**

Is all of the information that you need in the question?
The question tells you she saw one new movie every weekend over 6 weekends, or 6 new movies. It does not tell you the price of a movie ticket. The question does include a chart of movie ticket prices. You must find the price of a Saturday matinee ticket on the chart before you can solve the problem.

Is there extra information? **Yes. The chart tells you the other movie ticket prices. You only need the matinee price.**

Step 2: Make a plan.

This problem tells you that Erin went to see 6 new movies, and each ticket had cost $5.00. Problems that tell you a value for one item, and ask you to find a value for more than one of the same item are multiplication problems. Problems that use words such as *each*, *every*, *of*, *per*, *rate*, *times*, and *multiple* may be multiplication problems.

Multiply the number of tickets purchased (6) by the cost of each ticket ($5.00).

Step 3: Follow the plan.

Since $5.00 ends in zeros,
6 x $5.00 is the same as 6 x $5.

6 x $5 = $30

**Erin spent $30.00 over
6 weekends to see new movies.**

Step 4: Review.

Does the answer match the question?
**Yes. The problem asks for a
dollar amount.**

Check the answer.
**Multiplication problems can be
checked using repeated addition.
Add $5.00 for each week
Erin saw a new movie.**

$5.00
$5.00
$5.00
$5.00
$5.00
+ $5.00
$30.00

Drew's family bought 5 submarine sandwiches. They ordered extra cheese on 1/5 of the submarine sandwiches. How many of the sandwiches had extra cheese?

Step 1: Understand the problem.

Read the problem. Is there anything you do not understand?

What does the problem ask you to find?
How many of the sandwiches had extra cheese.

What information do you need to solve the problem?
The number of sandwiches purchased, and what fraction of them had extra cheese.

Is there any extra information? **No, there is no extra information.**

Step 2: Make a plan.

The word *of* in this problem indicates that it is a multiplication problem. "1/5 of" means "1/5 times." To find the number of sandwiches with extra cheese, multiply 1/5 and 5.

Multiplication Properties

Like the addition properties, multiplication properties can make problems easier.

The Associative Property: Changing the grouping of the factors does not change the product.

$$(4 \times 2) \times 3 = 4 \times (2 \times 3)$$

The Commutative Property: Changing the order of the factors does not change the product.

$$8 \times 7 = 7 \times 8$$

The Identity Property: The product of one and any number is the other number.

$$1 \times 32 = 32 \text{ and } 97 \times 1 = 97$$

The Inverse Property: The product of inverse fractions is 1.

$$(3/2) \times (2/3) = 1$$

The Zero Property: The product of any number and zero is zero.

$$62 \times 0 = 0$$

Step 3: Follow the plan.

The inverse property of multiplication says that when you multiply a number and its inverse, the result is 1. 5 is the same as 5/1, so 1/5 and 5 are inverses.

$1/5 \times 5 = 1$
One sandwich had extra cheese.

Step 4: Review.

Does the answer match the question?
Yes. The problem asked for a number of sandwiches.

Did the plan work for the problem? **Yes.**

Check the answer using multiplication without the inverse property. Is the answer the same? **Yes.**

A stand at the mall sells gold chains by length. Dana picked a style that cost $7.00 per inch. She bought 6.25 inches for a bracelet. Later, she went back and bought 8.75 inches for an ankle bracelet. What was Dana's total cost for the gold chains?

Step 1: Understand the problem.

Read the problem. Is there anything you do not understand?

What does the problem ask you to find?
The total cost for Dana's gold chains.

What information do you need to solve the problem? **The price of the chain per inch, and how many inches Dana purchased.**

Is there any extra information? **No, there is no extra information.**

Step 2: Make a plan.

More than one operation is indicated in the problem. The words *price per inch* indicate multiplication. There are two chains that were purchased, and the problem asks for a total. This indicates addition.

Let's break the problem into two parts to solve it.

Step 3: Follow the plan.

Since there are two lengths of the same style of chain, you can add the two lengths first.

6.25 + 8.75 = 15

Dana bought 15 inches of gold chain in all.

The cost per inch of the chain was $7.00. Multiply the price per inch by the total number of inches.

15 x $7.00 = $105.00

Dana's total cost for the gold chains was $105.00.

Step 4: Review.

Does the answer match the question?
Yes. The problem asks for a total cost, so the answer should be a dollar value.

Is the another way you can solve the same problem?
Yes. You can find the cost of the chain for the bracelet, and the cost of the chain for the ankle bracelet, then add the costs for a total.

Cost of the bracelet:
6.25 x $7.00 = $43.75

Cost of the ankle bracelet:
8.75 x $7.00 = $61.25

Total cost:
$43.75 + $61.25 = $105.00

This problem can be solved two different ways because of the distributive property.

In a multiplication problem, if one of the factors is a sum, you can add first, OR you can multiply each addend separately, then add the products. The answer is the same.

factor x factor
($7.00) x (6.25 + 8.75)
sum

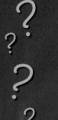

Amber downloads music from a pay-per-song Web site. She pays $0.99 for each song. On Tuesday, she spent $49.50 downloading songs. Use an algebraic equation to find the number of songs Amber downloaded on Tuesday.

Step 1: Understand the problem.

Read the problem. Is there anything you do not understand?

What does the problem ask you to find?
The number of songs Amber downloaded on Tuesday.

Do you have all of the information you need to solve the problem?
Yes. You know how much it costs to download one song, and the total amount Amber spent on downloading songs.

Does the problem ask for anything else? **Yes. You need to use an algebraic equation to find the answer.**

Step 2: Make a plan.

This problem tells you the plan. You must write an algebraic equation, then solve the equation to find the answer.

Step 3: Follow the plan.

Amber downloaded a number of songs for $0.99 each. This is a multiplication situation. Use words to tell what happens in the problem. Replace the words with numbers, symbols and variables. Use the variable s to represent the number of songs.

cost per song times number of songs = total cost

$$0.99s = 49.50$$

Divide each side of the equation by 0.99 to get the variable, s, by itself. Then do the division.

$$\frac{0.99}{0.99}s = \frac{49.50}{0.99}$$

$$s = \frac{49.50}{0.99} = 50$$

Amber downloaded 50 songs on Tuesday.

Step 4: Review.

Check your answer.
Write the algebraic equation and replace the variable with the solution.

$$0.99s = 49.50$$
$$0.99(50) = 49.50$$
$$49.50 = 49.50$$

Does your answer make sense?
Yes. $0.99 is very close to $1.00. If Amber downloaded 50 songs on Tuesday, and each cost her $0.99, the total should be close to 50 $\times$ $1.00, or $50.00. $49.50 is very close to $50.00.

A high school marching band has 72 members. When they march in a parade, there are six band members marching in each row. How many rows does the band form?

Step 1: Understand the problem.

Read the problem. Is there anything you do not understand? Does *rows* mean the number of people standing side by side, or front to back? **In this case, it is the number of people side by side. Items in rows are normally next to each other, and those in columns are above and below, or front to back. The meaning of row is NOT critical to the answer for the problem.**

What does the problem ask you to find?
The number of rows the band forms.

What information do you need to solve the problem?
The number of band members, and the number of band members in each row.

Is all of the information that you need in the question? **Yes.**

Is there extra information? **No.**

Step 2: Make a plan.

There are 72 band members that march in rows of 6. You can draw a picture of rows of six and count until you reach 72. Then you can count the number of rows.

Step 3: Follow the plan.

When you draw a picture to solve a problem, it does not have to be perfect. You can use an X to represent each band member. Draw rows with 6 Xs in each row. Count each X as you draw until you reach 72.

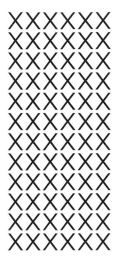

Count the number of rows. There are 12 rows.

The marching band forms 12 rows.

....

Step 4: Review.

Does the answer match the question?
Yes. The problem asked for a number of rows, and the answer is a number of rows.

Check the answer.
Count the number of rows in the drawing again.
Did you get the same number? Yes.

? Terri's cell phone is billed every 30 days. She is
charged for every text message she sends, but
not for those she receives. Her last bill showed
that she had 1,560 text message charges. On
average, how many texts did Terri send each day?

Step 1: Understand the problem.

Read the problem. Is there anything you do not understand?

What does the problem ask you to find?
The average number of text messages Terri sent each day.

What information do you need to solve the problem?
**The total number of messages Terri sent, and the total
number of days.**

Is all of the information that you need in the question?
**Yes. You know the number of messages sent from Terri's bill,
and know the bill covers 30 days.**

Is there extra information? **No.**

Step 2: Make a plan.

This problem tells you that Terri was billed for sending 1,560 text
messages over 30 days, and it asks that you find the average per
day. Problems that tell you a value (1,560 texts) for more than
one unit (30 days) and ask you to find a value for one of the
same unit (one day) are division problems. Problems that use
words such as *average, per, evenly, every, half,* and *shared* may
be division problems.

Step 3: Follow the plan.

Divide the number of text messages (1,560) by the number of days (30).

1,560 ÷ 30 = 52

Terri sent an average of 52 text messages each day.

Step 4: Review.

Does the answer match the question?
Yes. The problem asked for a number of text messages.

Check the answer.
Division problems can be checked using multiplication. Multiply the average number of messages per day (52) by the total number of days (30).

$$\begin{array}{r} 52 \\ \times\ 30 \\ \hline 1{,}560 \end{array}$$

Michael and his two friends bought a pizza and divided the cost equally. Each paid $5.00. Use an algebraic equation to find the cost of the pizza.

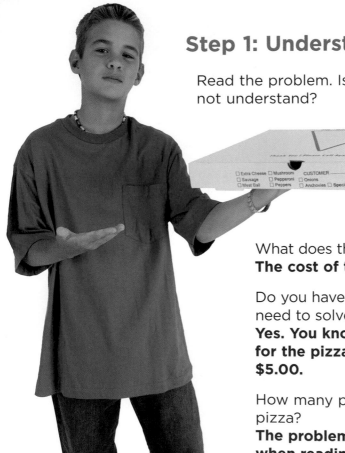

Step 1: Understand the problem.

Read the problem. Is there anything you do not understand?

What does the problem ask you to find?
The cost of the pizza.

Do you have all of the information you need to solve the problem?
Yes. You know how many people paid for the pizza and that they each paid $5.00.

How many people helped pay for the pizza?
The problem uses the number 2, but when reading carefully, there are 3 people, Michael and 2 friends.

Does the problem ask for anything else? **Yes. You need to use an algebraic equation to find the answer.**

Step 2: Make a plan.

This problem tells you the plan. You must write an algebraic equation, then solve the equation to find the answer.

....

Step 3: Follow the plan.

The price of a pizza is split equally among 3 friends. This is a division situation. Use words to tell what happens in the problem. Replace the words with numbers, symbols, and variables. Use the variable p to represent the price of the pizza.

cost of pizza divided by number of people = price per person

$$p \div 3 = \$5.00$$

Multiply each side of the equation by 3 to get the variable, p, by itself. Do the multiplication.

$$p \div 3 = \$5.00$$
$$p \div 3 \times 3 = \$5.00 \times 3$$
$$p = \$5.00 \times 3 = \$15.00$$

The cost of the pizza was $15.00.

....

Step 4: Review.

Check your answer.
Write the algebraic equation and replace the variable with the solution.

$$p \div 3 = \$5.00$$
$$\$15.00 \div 3 = \$5.00$$
$$\$5.00 = \$5.00$$

Does your answer make sense? Read the problem again to be sure you have the correct units.
Yes. In this problem, the question asks for a cost. Since the problem uses dollars, the answer should also be given in dollars.

Gwen was given $400 in gas cards as graduation presents. Each gas card had the same value. There were 8 gas cards in all. Use an algebraic equation to find the value of each gas card.

Step 1: Understand the problem.

Read the problem. Is there anything you do not understand?

What does the problem ask you to find?
The value of each gas card.

Do you have all of the information you need to solve the problem?
Yes. You know the total value of the gas cards and the number of gas cards.

Does the problem ask for anything else? **Yes. You need to use an algebraic equation to find the answer.**

Step 2: Make a plan.

This problem tells you the plan. You must write an algebraic equation, then solve the equation to find the answer.

Step 3: Follow the plan.

Gwen has $400 in gas cards, and each card has the same value. This is a division situation. Use words to tell what happens in the problem. Replace the words with numbers, symbols, and variables. Use the variable c to represent the value of each card.

total value divided by value of each card = number of cards

$$\$400 \div c = 8$$

When the variable is the divisor, it takes two steps to get the variable by itself.
First, multiply both sides of the equation by the variable.

$$\$400 \div c \times c = 8 \times c$$
$$\$400 = 8\,c$$

Then divide both sides by 8.

$$\$400 \div 8 = 8c \div 8$$
$$\$50 = c$$

Each gas card has a value of $50.

··

Step 4: Review.

Check your answer. **Write the algebraic equation and replace the variable with the solution.**

$$\$400 \div c = 8$$
$$\$400 \div \$50 = 8$$
$$8 = 8$$

You may write different words to tell what happens in this problem. The answer is always $50.

You could say:
total value divided by number of cards equals the value of each card
$$\$400 \div 8 = c$$

Or you could say:
number of cards times the value of each card equals the total value
$$8c = \$400$$

Use multiplication to check your division.
$$8 \times \$50 = \$400$$

James worked 2 six-hour shifts and 3 eight-hour shifts one week. He earns $7.50 per hour. Use an equation to find his gross pay for the week.

Step 1: Understand the problem.

Read the problem. Is there anything you do not understand? **What is gross pay? Gross pay is the pay you receive before taxes and other deductions are taken out. For an hourly job, multiply the number of hours worked by the pay per hour to find the gross pay.**

What does the problem ask you to find? **James's gross pay for the week.**

Is all of the information that you need in the question? **Yes. You know the number of hours James worked and his hourly pay.**

Step 2: Make a plan.

The problem tells you to write an equation to solve the problem.

Step 3: Follow the plan.

This problem uses more than one operation. You must first find the total number of hours that James worked, then multiply that number by his hourly pay. To write the equation, break it into parts. First write an expression for the number of hours James worked.

<u>**2 six-hour shifts plus 3 eight-hour shifts**</u>

$$2(6) + 3(8)$$

$$12 + 24$$

Use parentheses around the expression to multiply the total by the hourly pay.   **$7.50 (12 + 24)**

Use the order of operations to find the value of the expression. Write an equation using the expression, an equal sign, and the value.

$7.50 (12 + 24) = $270.00

James's gross pay for the week was $270.00.

Order of Operations

The **order of operations** is a set of rules that tells you which operations to do first.

1. Do operations inside **parentheses.**
2. Do **multiplication and division** in order from left to right.
3. Do **addition and subtraction** in order from left to right.

Step 4: Review.

Does the answer match the question?
Yes. The problem asked for gross pay, which is a dollar amount.

Check your math.
Did you do all of the operations correctly? Yes. Did you do them in the correct order? Yes

Multistep Algebra

Katie works at a local animal shelter on the weekends. On both Saturday and Sunday, the same number of dogs were adopted. There were 14 cats adopted on both days together. In all, 46 dogs and cats were adopted on the two days. Use an algebraic equation to find the number of dogs that were adopted on Saturday.

Step 1: Understand the problem.

Read the problem. Is there anything you do not understand?

What does the problem ask you to find?
The number of dogs that were adopted on Saturday.

Do you have all of the information you need to solve the problem?
Yes, you know the total number of animals adopted, the number of cats that were adopted, and that the same number of dogs were adopted on Saturday and Sunday.

Does the problem ask for anything else? **Yes. You need to use an algebraic equation to find the answer.**

Step 2: Make a plan.

This problem tells you the plan. You must write an algebraic equation, then solve the equation to find the answer.

Step 3: Follow the plan.

Write a sentence using the information in the problem.

<u>dogs adopted</u> <u>plus</u> <u>cats adopted</u> <u>equals</u>

<u>cats and dogs adopted</u>

You know the number of cats adopted, and the number of cats and dogs adopted together. Fill in those numbers.

dogs adopted + 14 = 46

Whenever it is possible, your variable should represent the value you are trying to find. You are trying to find the number of dogs that were adopted on Saturday. Let that be the variable s. The problem tells you the same number of dogs were adopted on each day, Saturday and Sunday, so the number of dogs adopted on both days must be $2s$.

$$2s + 14 = 46$$

Subtract 14 from each side of the equation.

$$2s + 14 - 14 = 46 - 14$$
$$2s = 32$$

Divide each side by 2.

$$2s \div 2 = 32 \div 2$$
$$s = 16$$

There were 16 dogs adopted on Saturday.

....

Step 4: Review.

Check your answer. **Try testing the answer in the context of the problem. If 16 dogs were adopted on Saturday, then 16 dogs were also adopted on Sunday, so 32 dogs were adopted on the two days together. Along with the 14 cats adopted, the total number of dogs and cats adopted in the two days was 32 + 14 = 46. This matches the problem.**

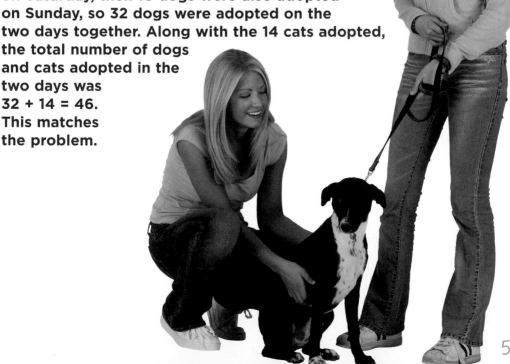

Write an inequality for the following sentence: You must be age 15 or older to get into the carnival without an adult.

Step 1: Understand the problem.

Read the problem. Is there anything you do not understand?

What does the problem ask you to find?
An inequality for the given sentence.

Do you have all of the information you need to solve the problem?
Yes.

Inequalities

An inequality compares two expressions using an inequality sign.

The inequality sign > means "greater than."

The inequality sign ≥ means "greater than or equal to."

The inequality sign < means "less than."

The inequality sign ≤ means "less than or equal to."

Step 2: Make a plan.

One way to understand an inequality is to draw a number line. Use the number line to decide which inequality sign is needed, then write the inequality using a variable.

Step 3: Follow the plan.

Draw a number line that includes the number 15.
Can you get into the carnival without an adult if you are 15? Yes.
Draw a solid circle on the number 15. A solid circle shows that
the number is part of the solution.

To get into the carnival without an adult, you must be 15 or older.
Show that the ages greater than 15 are included in the solution
by drawing an arrow from 15 over the values greater than 15 on
the number line. The number line is complete.

Choose a variable to represent the number or numbers for the
age of a person who can get into the carnival without an adult.
Let *a* stand for the age of the person.

The number line can help you understand what ages are included
in the solution. The age 15 and ALL ages greater than 15 are in
the solution set. The inequality sign is "greater than or equal to."

a ≥ 15

....

Step 4: Review.

Check your answer.
**The inequality says the
age is greater than
or equal to 15.
Is this what the
sentence in the
problem said?**
Yes, *15 or older* is
the same as *greater
than or equal to 15.*

In a math class, you must get at least 270 points on three tests combined for a grade of A. You get 86 on one test and 91 on another. What score do you need on the last test to earn an A?

Step 1: Understand the problem.

Read the problem. Is there anything you do not understand?

What does the problem ask you to find?
The score for the last test that will give you an A.

Do you have all of the information you need to solve the problem?
Yes. You know two of the test scores and the combined score you need to get an A.

Step 2: Make a plan.

The words "at least" in this problem tell you that you can use an inequality. Write and solve an inequality.

Step 3: Follow the plan.

Inequalities compare two expressions. For this problem, one of the expressions is the total of the three tests. The other is the number of points needed for a grade of A.
Write an expression for the total of the three tests. Let t equal the score on the third test.

$86 + 91 + t$

To receive an A, the total must be at least 270. Think carefully about the words "at least." They mean the lowest possible score for an A is 270. Anything greater than 270 will also give an A grade. The inequality symbol is "greater than or equal to."

86 + 91 + *t* ≥ 270

Solve the inequality.

$$86 + 91 + t \geq 270$$

Add 86 + 91.
$$177 + t \geq 270$$
Subtract 177 from each side.
$$177 - 177 + t \geq 270 - 177$$
$$t \geq 93$$

To receive an A, the last test score must be greater than or equal to 93.

....

Step 4: Review.

Check your answer.

**Test more than one value for an inequality.
First test a score of 93.**

**86 + 91 + 93 = 270
Will 270 points earn you an A? Yes.**

**The answer says "greater than or equal to 93."
Test a value greater than 93. Let's try 100.**

**86 + 91 + 100 = 277
Will 277 points earn you an A? Yes.**

You can add or subtract the same value from both sides of an inequality, just as you can for an equation.

Multiplication and Division
(27) Inequalities

The eighth grade is having walkathon to raise money for new computers. Each sponsor pledges one dollar for every lap the student walks. If a student walks 5 laps, how many sponsors would he or she need to raise more than $30?

Step 1: Understand the problem.

Read the problem. Is there anything you do not understand?

What does the problem ask you to find?
The number of sponsors a student needs to raise more than $30.

Do you have all of the information you need to solve the problem?
Yes. You know how many laps the student walks and that each sponsor gives the same number of dollars as laps.

Step 2: Make a plan.

The words "more than" in this problem tell you that you can use an inequality. Write and solve an inequality.

Step 3: Follow the plan.

For this problem, one side of the inequality is the number of dollars the student raises. The other side is the $30 goal.
To find the number of dollars, multiply the number of laps walked by the number of sponsors. Let s be the number of sponsors.

5s

The problem asks for more than $30. "More than" is another way to say "greater than."

5s > 30

Solve the inequality.
Divide each side by 5.

$$5s > 30$$
$$5s \div 5 > 30 \div 5$$
$$s > 6$$

The student must have more than 6 sponsors to earn more than $30.

Step 4: Review.

Check your answer.

Test more than one value for an inequality.
First test a value of 6 sponsors.

5(6) = 30
Is 30 more than 30?

No. Since the symbol > means more than, not equal to, test a value greater than 6. Let's try 7.

5(7) = 35
Is 35 more than 30? Yes.

You can multiply or divide the same positive value from both sides of an inequality, just as you can for an equation. To multiply or divide by a negative value, you must reverse the direction of the inequality sign.
$-2x > 6$ becomes
$x < -3$.

Kip has $65.00 to spend at a used game store. He buys a cable that costs $6.50. Each used game costs $13.00. Use an inequality to find the number of used games Kip can buy after buying the cable.

Step 1: Understand the problem.

Read the problem. Is there anything you do not understand?

What does the problem ask you to find?
The number of used games Kip can buy.

Do you have all of the information you need to solve the problem?
Yes. You know how much Kip can spend and how much each item costs.

Step 2: Make a plan.

The problem tells you to use an inequality.

Step 3: Follow the plan.

For this problem, one side of the inequality shows how Kip can spend his money. The other side is the amount Kip can spend. To show how Kip can spend his money, add the cost of the games to the cost of the cable. To show the cost of the games, multiply the cost of one game by the number of games Kip can buy. Let g be the number of games.

13.00g + 6.50

The problem asks for the number of games Kip could buy. Kip must have enough money, so the amount Kip spends must be less than the amount he has.

13.00g + 6.50 $<$ 65.00

Solve the inequality.
Subtract 6.50 from each side.
Divide each side by 13.00.

$$13.00g + 6.50 < 65.00$$
$$13.00g < 58.50$$
$$g < 4.5$$

Since Kip can buy only a whole games, you must decide what the inequality means. The inequality sign is "less than." The next lower whole number less than 4.5 is 4. Kip can buy 4 or fewer used games. This answer may be written many different ways, and be correct. For this problem, let's use the words "up to."

Kip can buy up to 4 used games.

Step 4: Review.

Does the answer match the question?
Yes. The problem asked for a number of used games. It also said to find the number using an inequality.

Check the answer.
How much will Kip spend if he buys 4 used games?
$13.00(4) + $6.50 = $58.50

How much will Kip spend if he buys 5 used games?
$13.00(5) + $6.50 = $71.50

Further Reading

Books

Abramson, Marcie. *Painless Math Word Problems.* Happauge, N.Y.: Barron's Educational Series, 2001.

Harnadek, Anita. *Algebra I Word Problems.* Seaside, Calif.: Critical Thinking Company, 2001.

McKellar, Danica. *Kiss My Math: Showing Pre-Algebra Who's Boss.* New York : Hudson Street Press, 2008.

Yang, Rong. *A-Plus Notes for Beginning Algebra: Pre-Algebra and Algebra 1.* Redondo Beach, Calif.: A-Plus Notes Learning Center, 2006.

More Math Help from Rebecca Wingard-Nelson:

Wingard-Nelson, Rebecca. *Algebra and Pre-Algebra.* Berkeley Heights, N.J.: Enslow Publishers, Inc., 2008.

Internet Addresses

Algebra.com. "Word Problems."
   <http://www.algebra.com/word-problems.mpl>

The Math Forum. "Ask Dr. Math" © 1994–2009.
   <http://mathforum.org/library/drmath/sets/mid_algebra.html>
   <http://mathforum.org/library/drmath/sets/mid_word_problems.html>

Index